BACKYARD WILDLIFE

Weasels

By Megan Borgert-Spaniol

BELLWETHER MEDIA • MINNEAPOLIS, MN

Note to Librarians, Teachers, and Parents:

Blastoff! Readers are carefully developed by literacy experts and combine standards-based content with developmentally appropriate text.

Level 1 provides the most support through repetition of high-frequency words, light text, predictable sentence patterns, and strong visual support.

Level 2 offers early readers a bit more challenge through varied simple sentences, increased text load, and less repetition of high-frequency words.

Level 3 advances early-fluent readers toward fluency through increased text and concept load, less reliance on visuals, longer sentences, and more literary language.

Level 4 builds reading stamina by providing more text per page, increased use of punctuation, greater variation in sentence patterns, and increasingly challenging vocabulary.

Level 5 encourages children to move from "learning to read" to "reading to learn" by providing even more text, varied writing styles, and less familiar topics.

Whichever book is right for your reader, Blastoff! Readers are the perfect books to build confidence and encourage a love of reading that will last a lifetime!

This edition first published in 2012 by Bellwether Media, Inc.

No part of this publication may be reproduced in whole or in part without written permission of the publisher. For information regarding permission, write to Bellwether Media, Inc., Attention: Permissions Department, 5357 Penn Avenue South, Minneapolis, MN 55419.

Library of Congress Cataloging-in-Publication Data
Borgert-Spaniol, Megan, 1989-
Weasels / by Megan Borgert-Spaniol.
    p. cm. – (Blastoff! Readers. Backyard wildlife)
Includes bibliographical references and index.
Summary: "Developed by literacy experts for students in kindergarten through grade three, this book introduces weasels to young readers through leveled text and related photos"–Provided by publisher.
ISBN 978-1-60014-725-8 (hardcover : alk. paper)
1. Weasels–Juvenile literature. I. Title.
QL737.C25B67 2012
599.76'62–dc23   2011028951

Printed in the United States of America, North Mankato, MN.

010112   1207

Contents

Weasels are small **mammals** with long bodies.

They live in **burrows** in logs and rock piles.

Most weasels
have brown fur
on their backs.
They have white
fur on their bellies.

Weasels blend in with leaves and rocks. This keeps them safe from owls, foxes, and other **predators**.

Most weasels **shed** their brown fur for winter. They grow white coats that blend in with the snow.

Weasels hunt
voles, mice,
and rabbits.

They follow their
prey into burrows.
Then they attack
by surprise!

Weasels also climb trees to find food. They take eggs from bird nests.

Weasels begin to hunt when they are two months old. This weasel caught a rabbit!

Glossary

burrows—holes or tunnels; weasels live in burrows.

mammals—warm-blooded animals that have backbones and feed their young milk

predators—animals that hunt other animals for food

prey—animals that are hunted by other animals for food

shed—to get rid of the outer layer of hair

voles—small rodents that look like mice; weasels hunt voles.

To Learn More

AT THE LIBRARY

Grant, Rose Marie. *Andiamo, Weasel!* New York, N.Y.: Alfred A. Knopf, 2002.

Morgan, Sally. *The Weasel Family.* North Mankato, Minn.: Cherrytree Books, 2004.

Shaw, Hannah. *Sneaky Weasel.* New York, N.Y.: Knopf Books for Young Readers, 2009.

ON THE WEB

Learning more about weasels is as easy as 1, 2, 3.

1. Go to www.factsurfer.com.

2. Enter "weasels" into the search box.

3. Click the "Surf" button and you will see a list of related Web sites.

With factsurfer.com, finding more information is just a click away.

Index

The images in this book are reproduced through the courtesy of: Ken Hoehn, front cover; tbkmedia.de / Alamy, p. 5; Konstantin Mikhailov / Minden Pictures, p. 7; Edwin Giesbers / Minden Pictures, p. 9; Tom & Pat Leeson / Kimballstock, p. 11; Ronnie Howard, p. 13; Konrad Wothe / Minden Pictures, p. 15 (top); Anna Kravchuk, p. 15 (left); Henry Wilson, p. 15 (right); Joe Blossom / Alamy, p. 17; Moodboard RF / Photolibrary, p. 19; Flip De Nooyer / Minden Pictures, p. 21.